#BAJANISMS

#BAJANISMS

A culture. A language.

Volume 1

MAHALIA CUMMINS

BRIDGETOWN BARBADOS

This book is available in print at most online retailers.
First Printing, 2020

ISBN 978-976-96341-1-4

www.bajanisms.com

CONTENTS

06

DE FIRST BEGINNING

07

SOUND AUTHENTIC

09

PRONUNCIATION

29

GREETINGS

35

SENTENCES

39

VERBS

43

RETRO
&
DECOMMISSIONED

47

WORD CONTRACTIONS

51

COLLOQUIAL

53

BAJANISMS: A LIST

DE FIRST BEGINNING

THE VERY START

The native language of the Barbadian people is English. The 'Queen's English', to be exact.

Yet, if one were to travel across Barbados, one would quickly notice something more prevalent among the people—our own rhyme and rhythm, our own Bajan Dialect.

Bajan, as we call it, is considered a dialect and not an official language. The history of dialects and Creoles in the Caribbean is long and complex and the linguistic background of Bajan dialect is no different. Bajan dialect, like other non-standard language varieties in the Caribbean—and across the world—does not have a standardised written code, yet it is as rich and vibrant as the languages that we consider 'official'.

To an unfamiliar ear, however, Bajan will almost certainly sound like a completely different language. *Bajanisms* is the term given to the unique elements of our dialect, as well as our embodiment of what it means to be Bajan.

What started as a social media hashtag blossomed into an overwhelming desire to share my culture with the world.

This book seeks to (re)introduce, enlighten and enamour the reader to a language I love, from the place I was born and raised and that will always be home.

Welcome to #bajanisms.

sound authentic

Most Caribbean accents can sound really similar but a few stand apart. The Bajan accent is one of them. I like to describe our accent as being a little less melodic and more on the percussive side—like drums.

It's proven quite challenging for people of other nationalities to successfully imitate our speech unless they have been thoroughly marinated in it—and sometimes not even then. So, some of you out there, prepare to have a rough go of it.

BAJAN:

PRONOUNCED

BAY-JUN

AND NOT

BAH-HAN

pronunciation

The way we pronounce words is super important and one of the things that makes Bajan stand out. It's true that there is no one way to spell most of our adaptations; however, throughout the book I have spelled out words phonetically for ease of pronunciation. There is also a pronunciation key at the end of the book to use as a reference for the IPA symbols used in *bajanisms: a list*. Here are some basics.

BASICS

We don't taper the ends of our words; rather, we often chop them right off for a blunt, matter-of-fact sound.

> e.g. Words like *way* are pronounced like the sound of Rihanna's 'eh' in the song *Umbrella* (ella, ella, eh, eh, eh).

We generally pronounce the hard 'R' sound—unless it's at the end of a word, in which case it gets the chop treatment. It then becomes a sound similar to the 'u' in *umbrella*.

> e.g. Words like *water* are pronounced like 'wau-tuh'.

We remove the 'g' sound from words ending in 'ing'. This may already be familiar.

> e.g. A phrase like *running out* is pronounced 'runnin' out'.

Words that begin with 'th' lose the 'h' sound.

> e.g. *Three* is pronounced 'tree'.

'Th' is also replaced with 'd' to begin certain words.

> e.g. *Them* is pronounced 'dem'.

While substitutions are prevalent in the first syllables, they can occur in any part of the word.

If 'th' occurs in the middle or at the end of a word, it may be pronounced 'f' or 'd'.

> e.g.   *Matthew* becomes 'Maffew'
> *Father* becomes 'fadduh'
> *Both* becomes 'boaf'

OOH LA LA!

Our national dish is coucou (and flying fish), which is a word that probably looks pretty French at first glance. The standard pronunciation (coo-coo) also sounds pretty French. But some Bajans change that first 'oo' to 'uh'. So *coucou* is pronounced 'CUH-koo'.

And so... *together* is pronounced 'tuhgedduh'.

That being said, *spoon* is still 'spoon' and *noon* is still 'noon'. However, *tune* is pronounced 'choon' and *tuna* may be pronounced 'choonuh', depending on the person.

ONE OR OWN

To indicate possession, we say a thing is in the ownership of someone or belongs to them. But the word *own* has evolved into 'wun'.

Hers/His == She/He wun
Ours == We wun
Theirs == Dem wun

Older Bajans may still use *own*.

We pronounce several words differently and those pronunciations must become a staple in your vocabulary if you want to sound authentic. They will be present in most, if not all, conversations with Bajans.

TING

We say 'ting' instead of *thing*. 'Ting' is also important because it can be used to represent any person, place, event, action or object.

> e.g. Man, he's *ting* last boy mannn. From cross dey in *ting*. He come to pick up de *ting* but when I *ting* it, it do de *ting*.

DOA

Though. Can be used in any way that *though* is used in standard English. Similarly, *although* becomes 'alldoa'.

'Doa' may also be used to punctuate the end of statements, repeated as a taunt and followed by 'nuh' for emphasis.

> e.g. I feel like gine sleep but I real howngry *doa*.
> Looka dis ting fuh me *doa* nuh.
> You kyan catch me *doa doa*.

Here are some other essentials for your arsenal.

A/Of/Have/I == Uh (In the case of *I* some of us interchange this pronunciation with the standard pronunciation.)

Could/Can == Kuh

Don't == Doan

For == Fuh

Go == Guh

Going == Gine

Isn't/Am not == Ain'/Ain't/Int/ Ent

It == Um

Me == Muh
(only as used in some phrases or sentences)
e.g. *Look for me tomorrow* becomes 'Look fuh *muh* tomor'.

It is I may become 'Is me' but never 'Is muh'. *Muh* may never be used on its own.

No/Please/Right? == Nuh

On == Pun/Pon

That == Dah/Dat

The == De (pronounced 'dee')

The person == De Body

There == Dey

They/Them/Their/They're == Dem

There are == Dem got

Us == We

What/Would/Well == Wuh (More on this in a bit.)

You all == Wunna

You/Your == You/Yuh

WUH?

The grammatical family of *wh-* question words provides a lot of necessary information. In Bajan, most of these words all boil down to one: 'wuh'. Bajans use 'wuh' to mean *where*, *what* and *which*.

Used as *what*:

> What are you doing? == *Wuh* you doin'?

Used as *where*:

> Where are you going? == *Wuh* part you gine?

Used as *which*:

> Which pen did you have? == *Wuh* pen you had?

We also interchange *what* and *which* in our speech at times, which is why 'wuh' works.

For example, some Bajans say '*Which* part you gine?' for *Where are you going?* This, in turn, can be further adjusted to '*Wuh* part you gine?'.

One should also note that *which* may be completely removed, making the phrase 'Part you gine?'.

Along with these uses, 'wuh' also means *well* and *would*. When used as *well*, 'wuh' is placed at the beginning of the statement or question.

Used as *well*:

      Well, you would have to know. == *Wuh* you wuh hahh know.

      Well then... or Well well... == *Wuh* heeyyyyyy...

'Wuh' can also be placed simultaneously in front of and behind a word to swiftly dismiss the mere thought of whatever was being implied.

e.g. Wuh money wuh?

'Wuh' is so versatile in Bajan that it is also used like 'Really?', 'Definitely!' or 'But of course!'. We also use the word *if* in this way.'Wuh'—but never *if*—may also mean 'Are you serious?'.

IF!?

'If' is sometimes said to prompt the repetition of speech that wasn't quite heard or understood. It can also be used to show agreement with or add emphasis to what the other person said.

e.g. Person A: De rain come down real hard dis morning.

    Person B: *IF?!* or *If* it come down hard?!

ON?

Bajans adjust the sound of 'un' at the beginning of the word *under* to 'aw' like the 'o' in *octopus*.

We will also remove the 'der' syllable or change it to 'duh'. We'll see more of this in Word Contractions.

Underneath becomes 'ohneat', 'onneat' or 'ondaneat'.

Some Bajans will still pronounce it with the 'uh' sound to get 'uhneat' or 'undaneat'.

Some may also replace 'th' with 'f' at the end of the word.

Underneath then becomes 'ohneaf', 'onneaf' or 'ondaneaf' and even 'uhneaf' or 'undaneaf'.

DAYS OF THE WEEK

Much like the first 'oo' in *coucou*, Bajans will adjust the 'ay' in *day* to the very widely used 'uh' sound when pronouncing days of the week.

The 'ay' may also be adjusted to 'ee', as in the first syllable in *evil.*

Monday == Mun-duh or Mun-dee

Tuesday == Chooz-duh or Chooz-dee

Wednesday == Wenz-duh or Wenz-dee

Thursday == Turz-duh or Turz-dee

Friday == Fry-duh or Fry-dee

Sunday == Sun-duh or Sun-dee

Saturday is special. This one has several different pronunciations across people and parishes.

Saturday == Sat-duh, Sat-dee, Sat-ta-day, Sat-ta-duh, Sarr-duh, Sarr-dee

MONTHS OF THE YEAR

Bajans use a combination of the rules in BASICS across our dialect. Similar to the days of the week, 'er' endings on months are pronounced 'uh'. Most months that are spelled with 'ry' at the end are pronounced without the final 'y' (ee), making them sound like they end with 'er'.

Here are the ones we say a bit differently:

January == Jan-yoo-werr/Jan-na-wer-ry

March == Mahrch

April == Eeyuh-prull

May == Me-yuh

June == Jyoon

July == Joo-lye

August == Aw-guss

September == Sep-tem-buh/Set-tem-buh

October == Oc-toa-buh

November == Noa-vem-buh

December == Dee-cem-buh/Duh-cem-buh

If you were wondering why February is missing, it is because February is unique. In Bajan, February has many forms.

February

==

Feb-ba-werr

Feb-ry

Feb-rer-ry

Feb-yu-erry

Feb-ba-wer-ry

Feb-yu-ry

PLIMPNUH

This title may look like a word made up by a toddler or something from a fictional story but, I assure you, it is something that exists to Bajans. We use the word to refer to an annoying grass burr that attaches to clothing and can give a sharp prick on the skin.

What is even more interesting is our numerous variations of this word.

plimp-nuh

plip-nuh

plimp-luh

prick-luh

plint-nuh

primp-luh

Some Foods

Avocado	Ah-fuh-kyad-duh
Breakfast	Brek-fus
Chewing gum	Tring gum
Chocolate	Chawk-lick
Coconut	Coat-nut
Lollipop	Lel-li-pop
Mangoes	Mang-gers
Pomegranate	Pown-gran-nit
Pumpkin	Pownk-kin
Sandwich	Sang-gridge
Shrimp	Strimps/Trimps/Skrimps
Tamarind	Tam-brin
Tomato	Tuh-mat-tuh
Turmeric	Tum-brick

Some Names

Brathwaite	Braf-fit/Braff-wit
Charles Rowe Bridge	Char-row Bridge
Cumberbatch	Kuhh-batch/Cum-ma-batch
Daniel	Dan-nil
Denise	Dee-nis/Den-neez/Dee-niece/Duh-niece
Grosvenor	Groze-nuh
Jonathan	Jawn-tun
Luther Thorne	Loo-fa-torn
Margaret	My-ee-grit/Mah-grit/Mah-ee-grit
Sharon	Shayrun/Shurrawn/Sharrn/Sharrun

Other Fun Pronunciations

Exactly	Ack-zack-ly
Athlete	Ah-fuh-leet
Umbrella	Am-bril-la
Alcohol	Ang-kuh-hall/Acka-hall/
	Ay-kee-hall
Ask	Anks
Another	A-nud-da/A-ned-da
Swimsuit	Bay-ding suit
Belongs to	Be-lonk-sta
Borrow	Borr
Bound	Bowng
Barbed wire	Cat-wehh
Supposed	Chup-pose
Children	Chur-ren/Tril-dren
Cloth	Clawt
Clothes	Cloaz
Spiderweb	Cow-web
Dominoes	Dahh-noes
Dwarf	Drawf
Duncy	Dump-sy/Downk-sy
Dynamite	Dun-na-mite/Dan-da-mite
Platform	Flat-farm
Film	Flim
Forehead	For-rid
Favorite	Fray-vrit
Funeral	Froon-rull
Gloves	Glubbs
Grandmother	Gran-murr/Gran-mud-da
Hang	Hing/Heng
Iron	I-run/Uhrrn
Encourage	In-kurge
Calculator	Kyah-kuh-lay-tuh
Car	Kyarr
Carry	Kyarr/Kyah
Shoelace	Lay-sun
Lightbulb	Light-bub

Little	Lil'/Lih-ya
License	Ly-sun
Mongoose	Man-goose
Married	Marrd
Millipede	Mel-la-pee
Medicine	Mel-son/Med-sin
Mercurochrome	Muh-cure-comb
Usual	New-jer-al
Use	Nuse
Unmannerly	Ohn-mar-ley
Opener	Ope-nuh
Alright	Ort
Ugly	Ow-gly
Poison	Pie-zun
Penguin	Ping-wing
Plaster of Paris	Plas-tuh pa-rish
Perfume	Puh-froom
Centipede	Saah-pee
Shouldn't	Shunn
Squeeze	Skreeze
Smooth	Smood/Smoov
Supermarket	Soo-ka-mar-kit
Say	Suh/Seh
Take care	Tek-kay
Toothpaste	Toos-pace
Treasure	Tred-jer
Throw	Truh/Tro
Tomorrow	Tuh-morr/Tuh-marr
Away	Way
Wouldn't	Wunn

For-rid

Chuh Back

Eye
Two Eye

Noaz

Mout

Chess

Bub-bies

Han'

El-buh

Han'
Two Han'

Pamm

Fin-guh

Nable

Nable String

Foot

Foot
Two Foot

Toaz

Shoal-duh

Teet

Teet

Box-cy
Bot-sy
Bot-bot
Bum-puh

greetings

'Manners maketh man' is a philosophy I—and many other Bajans—I grew up with and it can be seen across Barbados in the way we interact. It is expected that we exchange greetings as we pass each other, especially by our elders. The practice is so integral that as children, we may have been met with reprimand from our parents upon returning home because 'You see Miss Braffit today an' ain' speak?'

That being said, we greet our peers with unparalleled familiarity and younger Bajans cherish the greetings given by our elders.

HELLO

Inside! – This is used to get the attention of someone in a building instead of knocking.

Who de body is? == Who is it? (This can be used in person or over the phone.)

Wait, John, dah's you? == John, is it really you?

We may also just say a person's name or nickname or give a jovial descriptive announcement about them.

> Jooooohhhhhnnn?!
> Tallest?!
> A good man! A good man!

It's possible that the descriptive announcement may seem insulting or be quite profane in nature. However, these are usually said with love.

> John!! Yuh stinkin' crook!

WHO'S THERE?

When responding to any of these greetings, it's possible to be uncertain who you are speaking to, in which case the response is likely to be:

> Who de body is?

GOOD MORNING/AFTERNOON/EVENING

We often remove the 'Good' from the beginning of the greeting.

Some Bajans might also join the greeting to the 'Good' to make one word:

> Gummornin == Good morning
> Geevnin' == Good evening
> Gahftuhnoon == Good afternoon
> Gunnight == Good night

We also use 'Goodnight' as a greeting at night upon meeting someone or entering a space, as opposed to when parting ways or leaving.

Note: Some Bajans use morning at any time of the day, for fun, though our elders tend not to be fans of it.

HOW ARE YOU DOING?

Any of the following phrases is acceptable.

> Wuh gine on?
> Wuh um is? OR Wuh it is?
> How yuh keepin'?
> Yuh good?

GOODBYE

It's almost a certainty that a goodbye will start with our version of 'alright' or 'okay'. This also serves as an effective conversation ender.

> Ort!
> Ort good good!
> Ort I gine hey!
> Lata! OR Later on!
> I gone!

INTRODUCTIONS

While some of us say 'My name is...', there are lots of us who will just say 'I name [insert name]'.

Q: Wuh you name?

A: I name John.

In some scenarios, a bolder Bajan, who may be suspicious of or curious about your presence, will simply ask who you are instead of what your name is.

Q: Who's you?

A: I's John

sentences

The way Bajans form most sentences is much like standard English sentences are formed.

One big and important difference comes with the verb 'to be'. We will completely remove it in some cases, add it in others and even replace it with the verb 'to do'.

> *She brings water* becomes 'She is bring watuh' or 'She's bring watuh' or 'She does bring watuh'.

> *I am begging you* becomes 'Uh beggin' yuh'.

> *I am here* becomes 'I hey' while *I was here* becomes 'I did hey'.

> *I plant vegetables* becomes 'I is plant vegetables' or 'I does plant vegetables' and these both can become 'I's plant vegetables'.

This applies to questions as well.

> *What do you see?* becomes 'Wuh you see?'

We can also insert the verb 'to do' into a sentence that already has the verb 'to do' in it. This is known as *habitual does* in linguistics.

> *I do everything for her* becomes 'I does do everyting fuh she'.

> *What do you do?* becomes 'Wuh you does do?' or 'Wuh you's do?'.

QUALIFY & EMPHASIZE

Bajans qualify by placing the word 'real' before an adjective or adverb in a sentence instead of using 'really' or 'very'. We also emphasize by repeating words. The more a word is repeated, the greater the emphasis. For instance, something can be 'big big big', meaning it is very large.

'Real' may also be the repeated word. If 'real' is repeated, the adjective or adverb is not then repeated.

'You eat very quickly' may become:

'You does eat real fast.'
'You does eat real real fast.'
'You does eat fast fast fast.'

Another way we show emphasis is by using the words 'bare' or 'nuff'. 'Nuff' is adapted from 'enough' but is actually used to mean 'more than enough'.

You eat a lot of pumpkin may become:

'You does eat bare pumpkin.'
'You does eat bare bare pumpkin.'
'You does eat nuff pumpkin.'
'You does eat nuff nuff pumpkin.'

While 'real' qualifies verbs, adjectives and other adverbs, 'bare' is only ever used to qualify nouns as it replaces the phrase 'a lot of'. This means 'nuff' may also stand alone.

As a bonus, you may also use 'real' before 'nuff' for similar results but you may not use 'bare' in this way. In this scenario, the repeating word will ALWAYS be 'real' and NEVER 'nuff'.

You eat a lot may become:

'You does eat nuff.'
'You does eat real nuff.'
'You does eat real real nuff.'

REAL VERSATILE

While 'real' is generally used as a qualifier, it actually means 'actually existing as a thing or occurring in fact; not imagined or supposed'. So, when using it in this way, a Bajan will almost always add 'for' in front of 'real' to get 'for real', obviously with our pronunciation.

Something, someone or some scenario can be:

Fuh real   OR   Fuh real real

verbs

CONJUGATION

Let's talk conjugation! It doesn't really exist! Some words never change regardless of who or what they apply to. A good example of this comes from the verbs 'to be', 'to take' and 'to make'.

TO BE

I		
You		
He/She/It	==	Is
We		
You		
They		

TO MAKE

Note that in Bajan, 'make' and 'take' are pronounced 'mek' and 'tek'.

I		
You		
He/She/It	==	Mek
We		
You		
They		

TENSE

The continuous tense is usually formed by adding the suffix '-ing' to the word's infinitive form. *To be dead* would become 'deading' instead of *dying* and the continuous tense of 'mek' becomes 'mekkin'.

The future tense in Bajan often replaces 'will' with our contraction of the term 'am/is/are going to'.

I will make becomes 'I gine mek' or 'I gine and mek'.

The first of these two examples is used to imply an indefinite timeline, while the second implies the activity is likely already scheduled in and is close at hand.

In the future tense, the word 'now' is also important. 'Now' indicates the intention or implication that an action will be carried out as soon as possible.

We are about to do it becomes 'We gine do it now' or 'We doin' it now'.

'Now' may also indicate that an action was just completed.

I just did the dishes becomes 'I now wash de wares'. Yes, we say 'wares'. More on that later.

In the past tense, words seldom change their form from the infinitive. The familiar '-ed' doesn't exist—not even as a past descriptor. We may also insert 'was' or 'did' to indicate past continuous.

I made it yesterday becomes 'I mek it yestuhday'.
I did that becomes 'I do dah'.

OR

'I was mekkin' it yestuhday.'

Tossed Salad == Toss Salad
Baked Chicken == Bake Chicken

retro & decommissioned

Some terms are no longer in circulation but we dig them up from time to time to use ironically or for fun and nostalgia.

Short me crutch == A chronic lack of height

A pang == The most miniscule amount; an inconsequential amount

Barbagreen == Asphalt

Bariffle/Mobbatun == An exponential amount
See also *All branna*

Becausin' == Because

Blerk == The darkest black

Block == Cause or partake in a public confrontation

Bration == A date, a liason, a hookup.
Sounds like *nation*

Canniption/Conniption == A meltdown or tantrum

Effin/Iffin == If

Had was to == Was supposed to

Hobby/Hobby class == Without cost or payment; free

Leff muh lone == Leave me alone; stop bothering me

Lookuh muh crosses == I'm in complete disbelief

Lower up == Raise the volume

Mawlsprigg == Vigourously dismantle or consume

Me == My

On de slow boat to China == To act, calculate or understand something exceedingly slowly

Powful foolish == Unwavering and adamant in one's incorrectness or ignorance

Quick fast in a hurry == As quickly as possible

Screw pooch == An angry demeanour. One 'pulls' a screw pooch

Skipper/Starboy or Stargyurl == This is used to address anyone (even strangers) familiarly and with respect

Splurt == To vacate an area immediately and with swiftness

Try yuh effis best == Give your utmost

word contractions

Bajans have a talent for finding shortcuts. This is no different with our speech. Sometimes we'll find creative ways to say what we want with as little effort as possible.

A Bajan can join syllables, and even entire words, together to make them shorter. To those unfamiliar with our vernacular, that might very well make Bajan dialect sound even further removed from English.

Some fun contractions

A bundle of	A bun-luh
I am not	Ahhn
Amount of	A-monk-a
Better	Behh
Because	Caw
Come here	Cum-muh
That is it	Dahz-it/Dahz-um
The rest of it	De res-ser-it
Got to	Gaw
Give her/Give him/Give them	Gish-ee/Gih-ee/Gid-dem
Give us	Giw-we
Get out	Gyeh-owt
Have to	Hahh
Holler out for	Haw fuh
How do you mean	Hehh-meen
Ignorant	Ig-runt
Coming	Kehhn
Let go	Leg-go
Let us	Leh-we
A little bit	Lih-bit
Putting it/Put it	Puyn it/Peyt
Rubber bands	Ruhh banz
Stand up	Stahmp/Stan-nup
Starting motor	Starr moah
Trying it	Trehn it
Throwing it	Truyn it
Very wrong	Ver-rong
Well, I don't know	Wahh-no
Water	Wauh
Would have to	Wuh hahh

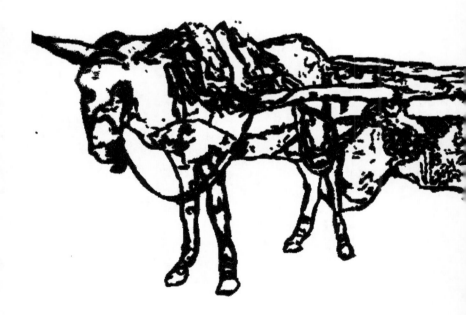

colloquial

Bajan is spoken at its best and most authentic in casual conversations among locals. Those who are unfamiliar may find it almost impossible to decipher the gist. The informality and creativity can be downright entertaining even to us but are essentially what add so much value to our everyday communication.

> For instance, if someone asks you 'You does work at Oran?' it means that you are blocking their view and must think that you are transparent. Oran is a local business that specializes in making windows.

UP UP & AWAY

> *Up* has a few uses in Bajan. Most popularly it is used after verbs in some of our expressions to indicate purposefully, thoroughly or completely.

For example:

> To trip == Trip up
>
> To lift == Liff up
>
> Scribble == Scrawl up

Up is also used directly in verb form in sentences where the required verb is implied by context.

> For instance, 'up it' may refer to raising volume, increasing intensity or even moving to a higher level.

bajanisms: a list

a cowboy

[ə kɒʊbɒɪ] · *noun*

The shortest shower imaginable; a sink bath. · One holds—and doesn't take—a cowboy.

*You I late and I ain bade yet. I gine gotta hol' **a cowboy** yuh.*

a drop

[ə drɒp] · *noun*

A lift in a vehicle. · Some Bajans do say 'a lift'.

*I want **a drop** cross by John.*

a lining cold

[ə laɪnɪŋ kol] · *noun*

A mysterious ailment caught if one sits on something damp or one goes outside 'in de dew'.

*Gyehp offa dah cold step 'fore yuh ketch **a lining cold.***

a mind

[ə maɪn] · *noun*

A Bajan's intuition. Usually mentioned when it was not followed. We may also use this to replace 'I figured' or 'I knew it!'.

A mind tell me bring my ambrilla caw de rain gine fall.

I had a mind de rain was gine fall.

I had a mind so!

a rushunn

[ə rʌʃʌn] · noun

A Russian. An individual who is constantly in a hurry or someone who needs instant gratification.

*Tek you time, you'z **a rushunn**?*

above/below

[əbʌv] / [bəlo] · prep

Situated next to, in front of or behind another location, object or person. Usually will mean neither *above* nor *below*.

*De house I lookin fuh just **above** or **below** de shop.*

ah?

[ā] · exp

This is used to convey sentiments such as 'I beg your pardon?', 'Are you being serious?' or 'Would you mind repeating?'.

Ah? You talkin' too soft man.

all branna

[ɒl branə] · exp

All brands of; a plethora; many varieties.

*Wunna talkin' **all branna** foolishness.*

55

all like now
[ɒl laɪk nɒʊ] ~ [ɒl nɒʊ] · adv
Immediately or already unfolding. May also be said 'all now'.
I would like some food all like now so.

alluhz
[alʌz] · noun
Aloe vera.
Uh want lil alluhz fuh put in muh hair.

as man
[az man] · exp
An expression used to guarantee the validity of any statement that is said before or after it.
I now see a sea monster down Miami Beach! As man!

at de door
[aʔ di dɔr] · exp
Completely exposed to any potential onlooker or observer.
Ehehh! Looka all she business at de door look!

at every cockfight

[aʔ ɛːvri kɒkfaɪt] · exp

Someone's attendance at what appears to be every event.

*Muh girl you does gaw be **at every cockfight**?*

bad feels
[ba: fiz] · exp
An ailment consisting of, but not limited to, extreme hunger, nausea and/or light-headedness. · One 'catches' bad feels.
*Lemme hol' a food before I catch **bad feels**.*

bandy
[bandi] · adj
Inaccurately aiming at, placing or situating oneself or an object. Crooked or askew.
*You! You park real **bandy** yuh!*

bandy foot
[bandi fut] · adj
Having bowlegs or knocked knees.
*Nuff footballers is be real **bandyfoot**.*

bark
[bark] · verb
To strike (or be struck) with extreme force using a projectile or blunt object.
*He mudda now **bark** he wid a lash.*

58

bassa bassa

[basə basə] · noun

A loud and often animated confrontation between parties. May result in a physical altercation or violence.

*You hear dem out in de road last night? It did bare **bassa bassa**!*

behh has

[bɛː haz] · exp

Should. This means that something is in your best interest.

*Wunna **behh has** guh long home.*

bim

[bɪm] · noun

a) Bin or wastepaper basket. This called a garbage/stuff bim.
b) Another name for Barbados; short for Bimshire.
c) A soft drink brand that used to be sold in Barbados.

*Truh dis hey in de stuff **bim** fuh me.*
*Yuh's only get Chefette in **Bim**.*
*Wunna ever had a baby **Bim**?*

blacklead
[blaklɛd ~ blaklɪd] · *noun*
Pencil.
*I waan write dis ting wid hey a **blacklead**.*

blige
[blaɪʤ] · *adj*
To have need of or to be obliged.
*I ain' **blige** fuh nuh shopping bag. I bring my wun from home.*

blista bline
[blɪstə blaɪn] · *verb*
To verbally denigrate or to be verbally denigrated with unparalleled intensity.
*I gine get **blista bline** fuh getting' home late.*

boa/boazie
[bo] / [bozi] · *exp*
Used to indicate that one has washed one's hands of a situation or declined from engaging further or at all.
*Not me **boa**!*
*I gine in my house **boazie**.*

bowng

[bɒʊŋ] · verb · adj

Severe constipation. The opposite of when something 'work yuh'.

*If you eat all dem achkees dem gine **bowng** yuh.*
*Yuh was in de bathroom long long like yuh **bowng**.*

bread n' two

[brɛd (a)n tu] · noun

A Bajan saltbread with two (or more) Bajan fishcakes as filling.
*I gine buy a **bread n' two** fuh lunch today.*

brek off yuh neck

[brɛk ɒf jə nɛk] · exp

Do everything in one's power to see something.
*Yuh gine **brek off yuh neck** to look at she?*

bruggadowng

[brʌɡədɒʊŋ ~ brʌɡədʌŋ] · exp · ideophone

The actual or implied sound of an object or person falling and hitting a hard surface with force.
*He trip ova a rock and hit de road, **bruggadowng**!*

61

breeze

[briz] · *verb*

Chill; relax; hang out; calm down. One may also 'breeze out' or be told to 'breeze yuh head'.

*We gine an' **breeze** down Browne's Beach.*

cat piss and peppa

[kat pɪs an pɛpʌ] · *exp*

A most heated confrontation; verbal altercation that may escalate to a physical fight.
It gine be **cat piss and peppa** *if two ah dem cross one anudda.*

catspraddle

[kjaʔspradəl] · *adj*

Lain to waste; to fall awkwardly and land in a dishevelled manner.
He trip ova a rock and all he tings was **catspraddle** *all cross de road.*

cheese on bread

[tʃiːz ɒn brɛd] · *exp*

An expression of exclamation such as 'Oh wow', 'Oh no' or even 'Oh yes'. The most requested expression a Bajan is asked to say while abroad.

come-tuh-muh
[kʌmtʌmʌ] · *noun*
A concoction that is thought to be used as an aphrodisiac or
love potion.
*Yuh like yuh get some **come-tuh-muh** put in yuh food.*

crappo
[krapo] · *noun*
Our adaption of *crapaud*, the French for 'toad'.
*De **crappos** went to sea.*

crumpsy
[krʌmpsi] · *adj*
Extremely crispy or crunchy.
*I like dem biscuits. Dem real **crumpsy!***

cuhdear
[kʌdeɪr] · *exp*
An expression of pity, sympathy or understanding. Used
similarly to 'poor thing', 'aww', 'how sweet' or 'isn't that cute'.
Cuhdear! He look suh tired doa.

cutter

[kʌtə]· noun

A saltbread filled with ham, fish, cheese or liver.
No other combination of a saltbread and filling is considered a cutter.

*Pink Star is mek de best liver **cutter** in Bim!*

dah easy
[da izi] · exp
That is no problem at all.
See also Doan watch nein.

dah fuh lick yuh
[da fə lɪk jʌ] · exp
It serves you right; you were asking for it;
you got what was coming to you.
Yuh wun buy dem tickets early now all gone. **Dah fuh lick yuh.**

dah sorr way
[da sɔr weɪ] · exp
That sort of way. Used to stress one's feelings on a subject.
I ain checking fuh wuh you tellin' me **dah sorr way** *doa.*

dangerous
[deɪndʒrʌs] · adj
Having the tendency to spread rumours and falsehoods or sow
mistrust.
Wunna too malicious and **dangerous.**

dark eye(s)

[dɑrk aɪz] · *exp*
The point of near loss of consciousness, usually due to hunger.
*You got any food? Hey gettin' lil' **dark eyes**.*

de belly

[di bɛli] · *noun*
Stomachache or upset stomach; diarrhoea.
*Dah maynaze gih yuh **de belly**?*

de honest troof

[di ɒnɪs trufl] · *exp*
The truth, the whole truth and nothing but the truth.
*Uh gine tell yuh de **honest troof**. I like yuh.*

de light burning

[di laɪt bɛrnɪŋ] · *exp*
The light (is) on. Used for any kind of light, even an LED.
*How you gine out and leff **de light burning**?*

de dog dead/shop shut/cock done crow
[di dɒg dɛd] / [di ʃɒp ʃʌt] / [di kɒk dʌn kro] · *exp*
It's already over or it's too late; that ship has sailed.
See also Gone tru de edduhz.
*Wait you now come fuh food? Wuh **de dog dead**.*

dey so look
[deɪ so lʌk] · *prep*
Regard that item or area within viewing distance.
*Look de ting I did want **dey so look**.*

doan watch nein
[don wɒtʃ nɛɪn] · *exp*
An indication not to worry. Used similarly to 'that's alright' or
'no worries'. May be replaced with 'dah small'.
See also Dah easy.
*Keep de change man, **doan watch nein**.*

do de dog/cat/puppy
[du di dɒg] / [du di kja?] / [du di pʌpi] · *exp*
To behave in a manner worth recounting the following day; to
lose oneself in the thralls of indigenous dance.
*Yuh **do de dog** in dah fete Satdee man!*

do

[du] · *exp*

Placed at the end of any suggested action to emphasise persuasion of one's self or others.

*Try an' eat de lil food **do**. 'Fore yuh get dark eyes.*

ehehh

[ɛhɛ:] · *exp*

An exclamation of shock and disbelief. The longer this is stretched, the more one indicates the level of disbelief being experienced.

Ehehhhhh! You wuh he now say?

ess

[ɛs] · *noun*

News; an interesting story; juicy gossip. The equivalent of the African-American Vernacular English use of 'tea'.

*Come lemmuh gih yuh dis **ess**, do.*

ess out

[ɛs ʊt] · *verb*

To leave a location.

*Come lewwe **ess out**, do.*

every long time sense

[ɛvri lʊʊ taɪm sɛns ~ ɛvə sɛns] · *adv phr*

Ever since; the period of time since; indication that a long time has passed. Bajans may also say 'ehhva sense'.

*I done do dah ting **every long time sense.***

eyes in eclipse
[aɪz ɪn iklɪps] · *exp*

Implying someone has missed the point or literally didn't see something that is right in front of them.

*Wait! De ting right dey! Yuh **eyes in eclipse** or wuh?*

fall downg

[fɒl dɒuŋ] · *verb*

Bajans don't just fall—we 'fall down'. And, if we trip over something and fall as a result, whatever we tripped over 'fall we downg'.
Any pronoun may replace 'we' in the above phrase.
Look! I now see a man **fall downg** *so hard!*

fall way

[fɒl weɪ] · *verb*

To have drastically and inexplicably lost weight.
This has a negative connotation.
Wait you sick? Yuh **fall way** *very bad.*

flex

[flɛks] · *noun*

A planned or unplanned outing with the potential for a favourable outcome.
We still mekkin' dah **flex** *tonight?*

frig way

[frɪg weɪ] · *verb*

To throw with great aggression or carelessness.
I done **frig way** *dah parking ticket.*

fussy

[fʌsi] · adj

To be excited, whether in anticipation of something to come or as a result of an experience.

*I now get a puppy and I so **fussy**.*

fyah-guh-lash

[faɹjʌɡəlaʃ ~ fɛːɡəlaʃ] · noun

An overtly passionate, spirited and boisterous individual.

*She does get on like a real **fyah-guh-lash** when she ready.*

get and
[gɛ(ʔ) an] · *exp*
To have 'gone and' done something. Often used when reprimanding or expressing surprise or annoyance due to something someone has done.
*Wunna **get** in hey **and** do bare foolishness yesterday.*

get (de) ridduh
[gɛʔ di rɪdə ~ gɛʔ rɪdə] · *verb*
To get rid of. If the following word begins with a vowel (or vowel sound), we marry it to the phrase using a hard 'R' sound.
Get de ridduh dis. Or *Get de ridderit.*

get me sick/get me tired
[gɛʔ mi sik] / [gɛʔ mi taɪjərd ~ gɛʔ mi tərd] · *exp*
To be the source of exasperation. Often used in jest.
*Wunna does **get me sick**!*

gone bum
[gɒn bʌm] · *exp*
Is no longer functioning. Usually mechanical or electronic devices.
*De TV **gone bum**.*

goosey
[gusi] · adj
Hazel or blonde. Usually hair or eye colour.
*Part you get dem **goosey** eyes from?*

gone clear
[gɒn kleɪr] · exp
To complete or excell at any task or activity; to receive a reward, award or accolade.
*Only two more runs and de Windies **gone clear**!*

gone tru de edduzz
[gɒn tru di ɛdʌz] · exp
Gone through the eddoes; means that something is a foregone conclusion or a moot point or no longer relevant. It may also mean that something is destroyed beyond repair.
*People nowadays like dem standards **gone tru de edduzz**.*

grabble
[grabəl] · verb
To hold on tightly and with no indication of release.
*Yuh got dah bag **grabble** up very tight!*

gree
[gri] · *verb*
To be amicable and generally friendly with someone.
*Wait! De two ah dem doan **gree**? All dis time I thought dem*
greeing.

gree back
[gri bak] · *verb*
Reconciliation that occurs after a fallout.
*Uh wonder if dem gine eva **gree back**.*

gully boar
[gʌli bɔr] · *noun*
An individual who aggressively forces their way, literally or
figuratively, with little to no regard for others.
*You now push tru dem people like a real **gully boar**.*

had a mind
[had ə maɪn] · *verb phr*
We use this phrase in place of saying 'that's what I thought' or 'I figured'. It may also stand alone.
I had a mind you was a tief!
I had a mind so!

hah-fuh
[hafʌ] · *exp*
A half of. Sometimes used to intensify an insult.
Gimme hah-fuh you tambrin ball, yuh hah-fuh idiot.

hard ears
[hard eɪrz] · *adj*
To be stubborn, disobedient or troublesome.
Hard ears yuh wun hear? Own way yuh gine feel.

hey so look
[heɪ so lʌk] · *prep*
Within immediate vicinity.
I got dah ting you did want right hey so look.

hol' ova/hol' up

[hol ovə] / [hol ʌp] · *verb phr*
Bend over/Cease bending over.
Wuh happen yuh hol' ova so? Hol' up 'fore de blood guh to yuh head.

how it stop/stan/stay?

[hoʊ ɪt stɒp] / [hoʊ ɪt stan] / [hoʊ ɪt steɪ] · *exp*
What condition is the structure, object or situation in?
De ting fall off de table? How it stop?

I sleep at you
[aɪ slip at ju] · *exp*
This question is posed to a person who hasn't offered a polite greeting upon seeing someone for the first time that day.
Wait!? I at sleep at you?

igrunt
[ɪ(ŋ)grʌnt] · *adj*
Clueless, deliberately reckless, aggressive or without regard for others. Describes someone who is the source of much entertainment.
He real igrunt yuh!

in at me
[ɪn at mi] · *exp*
At my house; on my property. Or simply 'at me'.
I kuh do as I like in at me.

in potta
[ɪn pɒtʌ] · *exp*
In a troublesome situation; a scenario that will have an undesirable outcome.
I ain revise fuh dah test. I gine be in potta tomor.

in two twos

[ɪn tu tuz] · exp

A measurement of time; the expeditious completion of any action, journey or scenario.

*I gine be done dis **in two twos**.*

jipsy
[ʤɪpsi] · *adj*
Intrusively curious about other people's affairs.
Also considered a slur internationally, due to its initial use to describe the Romani Gypsies.
Mind yuh business! Yuh too jipsy.

jobby
[ʤɒbi] · *noun*
Literal or figurative excrement; utter nonsense.
I now write bare jobby in dah essay.

***

kuh wells
[kə wɛlz] · *exp*
Could as well.
Wunna kuh wells guh long home. Everyting done.

leff out me/leff me out
[lɛf mi ʊt] · exp
Don't involve or implicate me; leave me be.
*Who meee? Not me soul, **leff out me**.*

liard
[laɪ(j)erd] · adj
Describing one who has the propensity to speak untruths.
*He so **liard** den!*

lick down
[lɪk dɒʊŋ] · exp
To strike or to be struck with force and subsequently succumb to gravity.
*You near get **lick down** by dah car.*

lick up
[lɪk ʌp] · adj
The result of 'getting lick down'; a state of near complete bewilderment, fatigue, disbelief or impairment.
*Dah workout got me **lick up**!*

lick yuh mout
[lɪk jʌ mɒʊʔ] · exp
The act of incessant talking or endlessly carrying on a conversation.
*Wunna ain tired **lickin' wunna mout**?*

lickrish
[lɪkrɪʃ ~ [lɪkrʌʃ] · adj
Gluttonous and greedy when it comes to food.
*Stop beggin'! Yuh too **lickrish**.*

long out
[lɒʊŋ ɒʊt] · verb
The action of sticking one's tongue out.
*You always gotta **long out** you tongue so when you wukkin' up?*

loody
[ludi] · adj
Ill-fitting due to looseness from being oversized or worn.
*Look how **loody** he ondawear is.*

lookuh

[lʊkʌ ~ lʊkə] · *exp*

Look here. Usually used to indicate that it is in the best interest of the listener to pay attention or take caution. Also used as an indication of disbelief at something seen.

Lookuh wuh gine on dey look.

malicious
[məlɪʃʌs] · adj
Deliberately prying into other people's affairs.
*Wunna too **malicious** and dangerous.*

marl hole
[marl hol] · noun
A place where everything emerges ashy and dry or a place
where neither cream nor lotion exist.
*Yuh want lil' cream? Look like yuh come out de **marl hole**.*

mind
[maɪn] · verb
To pay attention to; to be influenced by; watch, imitate, move, or
be cautious. Often paired with 'yuhslef', 'yuh friends', 'stupid
people', 'wuh yuh say or do', etc.
*Get and **mind** yuh friends and see wuh happen.*

miss and
[mɪs an] · exp
To do something accidentally.
*I **miss and** hit he.*

mistake and
[mɪsteɪk an] · *verb*
To make an error in judgement resulting in an unwanted result.
I mistake and open dah message.

mock
[mɒk] · *adj*
To imitate; false or fake; a replica.
Dah chain gaw be mock.

mock mock
[mɒk mɒk] · *exp*
Imaginary.
I was only doing it fuh mock mock, not fuh real real.

mock sport
[mɒk sport] · *exp*
Actual joking around; being a jester or fool.
You like tummuch mock sport.

mocka mocka
[mɒkʌ mɒkʌ] · exp
A perpetrator of imitation.
You'z a bare **mocka mocka**.

mogey
[mogi] · adj
An odour rife with dampness.
De rain wet dese clothes? Dem smell very **mogey**.

mole
[mol] · noun
Dirt or soil.
The name of a bashment soca artist.
Uh want lil **mole** *fuh de garden.*

moojin
[muʤɪŋ] · noun
A fool or silly individual.
Doan listen to he, he's a **moojin**!

mout like rock
[mɒʊʔ laɪk rɒk] · exp
Disagreeable, strong headed and mischievous. One may also be described as 'hard mout'.
Yuh mout like rock.

mussy
[mʌsi] · exp
Maybe; probably; likely; must be; has got to be.
He ain answer de phone? He han' mussy full.

nah-nee
[naːni] · adj
Anything that can be considered dirty or disgusting.
*Uh uhh! Dah look **nah-nee**.*

neckskin to nuttin
[nɛkskɪn tə nʌt(ɪ)n] · adj
Being half-naked.
*How you walking bout so wid **neckskin to nuttin** pun yuh?*

nippy
[nɪppi] · adj
Extremely short; usually refers to clothing.
*Wuh'z dis **nippy** skirt yuh got on?*

ning nong
[nɪŋ nɒʊŋ] · noun
A seemingly daft person.
*Dah mek sense to you, yuh **ning nong**?*

no please

[no pliz] · *exp*

Bajans may say this instead of 'no, thank you'.
Also used as an objection or to shut down unwanted attention or inclusion.

Be in who videa? **No please**, *not me and dat.*

obzocky
[ɒbzɒki] · *adj*
Awkward or abnormal in appearance.
*Dah cake you bake come out real **obzocky.***

on it/off it
[ɒn ɪt] / [ɒf ɪt] · *verb*
Turn it on./Turn it off.
*De TV off? **On it** dey so fuh me.*

oanliest
[onli(j)ɪs] · *adj*
Just plain 'only', although it may not be used in every way that
'only' is used. Only used before nouns.
For a statement like *The only thing I can say is no* one may say
*'De **oanliest** ting I kuh say is no'.*
For a statement like *I only said that to him* one may **not** say *'I
oanliest say dah to he'.*
Note that 'oanlier' is not a thing.

onpick yuh teet
[ɒnpɪk jʌ tit] · *exp*
To open one's mouth to speak
*You ain gine **onpick yuh teet** to say mornin'?*

o-pit-in
[opɪtɪn] · verb
Open it.
One may indicate a specific item. It then becomes 'Ope-dah-in'.
See dah bottle uh seeznin'? **oap-it-in** *fuh me.*

or wuh
[ɔr wʌ] · exp
Or what. Used to confirm agreement, often rhetorically.
You'z a moojin **or wuh?**

ort you
[ɔrt ju] · exp
Used similarly to 'if you say so'.
Used to indicate scepticism, sarcastic encouragement or
dismissal.
You and Rihanna went where? **Ort you.**

pick out
[pɪk ʊʊt] · verb
To successfully scope out, identify or hit a target from a great
or significant distance.
*How you get me **pick out** suh good from dah crowd?*

picky
[pɪki] · adj
Extremely short. Usually refers to hair length or clothing.
*I remember when my hair used to be **picky picky**.*

piss parade
[pɪs pəreɪd] · verb
To administer a severe and boisterous tongue-lashing.
*Uh hear yuh get home an' **piss parade** all tru de house.*

poor great
[por greɪt] · adj
Acting as though one is above or better than others, with no
basis for such behaviour.
*Since when you does get on suh **poor great**?*

poppit
[pɒʊpɪt] · noun
Someone who has proven to be severely lacking in intelligence or common sense. Someone who can be quite silly.
*You gine be a **poppit** all de days uh you life?*

porakey
[poreɪki] · adj
Appearing to be severely lacking in nourishment.
*Dah shirt suh loose it does got me lookin' real **porakey**.*

pritty pritty
[prɪti prɪti] · adv
Pretty.
The description of any action completed with grace and skill.
*He out dah batsman **pritty pritty**.*

pritty kulluh
[prɪti kʌlʌ] · adj
Multicoloured.
*I feel I gine put on dis **pritty kulluh** dress.*

puhtickluh and
[pətɪklʌ an] · *exp*
Particularly. Specifically, with intent.
I puhtickluh and tell you do dah ting.

put food
[pʊt fud] · *verb phr*
To plate food for consumption.
You want me put food fuh you or you gine put it?

reverse back
[rɪvərs bak ~ rəvərs bak] · *verb*
Just plain old reverse.
You got nuff space behind de cyar. **Reverse back** *lil' mo'.*

rumfle up
[rʌmfəl ʌp] · *adj* · *verb*
Wrinkled or dishevelled, specifically when referring clothing or a hairdo. Wrinkled clothing can also be referred to as 'rough dry'.
Sitting down in dis ZR gine **rumfle up** *all my clothes.*
Dis strong wind got my hair real **rumfle up.**

screw
[skru] · adj
Vexed.
One can be 'blue vex', which is an extreme level of vexation.
*Yuh lookin' very **screw** cross dey, wuh happen?*

self
[sɛlf] · exp
Emphasizes a specific moment in time.
*I talk to he today **self**.*

skimpy
[skɪmpi] · adj
Very revealing as it pertains to clothing.
Measley.
*Wuh's dis lil' **skimpy** piece of macaroni pie?*

skin a cuffin
[skɪn ə kʌfɪn] · verb
Do a forward roll, somersault or tumble.
*You know how to **skin a cuffin**?*

skin up
[skɪn ʌp] · exp
Contortion, dismantling or casting away of someone or something. One may skin up 'yuh face' or 'de whole apple cyart' or one can simply 'skin up', which would mean they have fallen.
My fren', yuh face very skin up!

skin teet
[skɪn tit] · noun · verb
To grin or to laugh out loud.
Every skin teet ain' a laugh.
You gine skin you teet all de time so?

sousey
[sɒʊsi] · adj
Indicates obesity.
May also indicate an undesirable outcome, state or attitude.
Santa Claus belly jolly or he just sousey?

sponge
[spʌnʤ] · verb
To take advantage of another's generosity without compensation or gratitude.
Uh uh. You kyahn sponge offa me at de shop today.

stay up
[steɪ ʌp] · verb
Stand up.
Stay up hey next to me and behave.

stirrin
[stər(ɪ)ŋ] · exp
Anything that's going around or trending—from an illness to infection or even pregnancy.
Careful. I hear dengue stirrin.

stoppuh
[stɒpʌ] · noun
Specifically refers to a bottle cap.
Watch yuh doan step pun dah stoppuh.

straight pull
[streɪt pʊl] · verb
Consume an entire beverage in one attempt.
Tall man now straight pull he whole rum n' coke!

strike back
[straɪk bak] · exp
To possess a feature from an elder or ancestor that hasn't
been present for a few generations.
*Part you get dem goosey eyes from? You **strike back**?*

stuff
[stʌf] · noun
A combination of dust, grass, leaves and any other debris,
including garbage.
*Everyday so wunna gine burn **stuff**?*

suh-warryuh
[səwɒr(i)jʌ] · noun
Someone who is notably combative.
Likely adapted from 'Sioux Warrior'.
*You always ready. You'z a **suh-warryuh** or wuh?*

swapsy
[swɒpsi] · adj
Having abundant, loose, mobile fat.

swibbly
[swɪbli] · adj
Having a loose and shrivelled up appearance; resembling a raisin or prune.

swing
[swɪŋ] · verb
To visit briefly, usually in a vehicle.
Swing fuh me to guh to de ting lata.

syduh
[saɪdə] · adj
Beside; next to.
Stannup hey syda me.

tek it light
[tɛk ɪt laɪt] · *exp*
A warning to be wary of potential consequences.
Alright you tek it light.

tie tongue
[taɪ tʊn] · *exp*
Used to describe someone who is having trouble speaking due to nervousness. Also used to describe any speech impediment, unless it's a stutter or stammer.
Often said to indicate that the hearer is having great difficulty understanding the speaker.
Wuh's dah yuh say? Yuh talkin' like yuh tie tongue.

tie up
[tai jʌp ~ tɛ:p] · *exp* · *adj*
A state of confusion or being mistaken or incorrect.
The state of one's mouth after consuming extremely sour, acidic or bitter food or drink.
Doan get tie up.

unfair
[ɒnfeɪr] · *verb*
To bully. To be bullied is to 'get unfair'.
*You ain gine stop **unfair** dah boy?*

up de ting
[ʌp di tɪŋ] · *exp*
To take any scenario or situation to the next level.
*Rihanna does just **up de ting** all de time!*

up to now
[ʌp tə nɒʊ] · *exp*
Used in negative statements to describe a situation that has existed up to this point or up to the present time.
*Whole day gone and **up to now** you ain bade?*

wait now
[weɪt nɒʊ] · exp
Very similar to 'Ort you!'. Used to indicate being taken aback by
an observation or upon receiving some information; giving an
individual or group encouragement.
May also be said as 'Wait boa!'.
Wait now! De day after Kadooment is a bank holiduh!

wares
[weɪrz] · noun
Ceramic tableware.
We don't say 'wash the dishes', we say 'wash de wares'.

was to
[wɒz tə] · exp
The current version of 'had was to' meaning 'was supposed to'
or 'meant to'. May also be said as 'did to'.
I was to call you last Satduh.

we does pitch marbles

[wi dəz pɪtʃ marbəlz] · exp

To be close friends. If this is posed as a question, it implies that the hearer and speaker are, in fact, not close friends.

*He bout dey talking bout me like **we does pitch marbles**.*

you
[ju: ~ ju ~ jʌ] · *exp*

While 'you' is interchanged with 'yuh' in regular speech, a Bajan will exclaim 'You!' instead of saying someone's name, to get someone's attention, or to express delight or disdain regarding something they are about to share, heard, witnessed or remembered.
'You' is also lengthened indicate disbelief or shock.
The longer the word is drawn out, the more shock or disbelief is being experienced.
You! Stop dat!

✽✽✽

pronunciation key

VOWELS

Phonetic Symbol	Key Word
i	beat
ɪ	bit
eɪ	bait
ɛ	bet
ʌ	but
ə	buh-bye
a	bat
aɪ	bite
ɑ	bark
ɒ	bob
ɒʊ	bout
ɒɪ	boy
o	boat
ɔ	born
ʊ	book
u	boot

CONSONANTS

Phonetic Symbol	Key Word
b	bat
tʃ	chat
d	dog
f	fan
g	get
h	hat
dʒ	jam
k	kite
l	lip
m	man
n	nap
p	pan
r	run
s	sun
ʃ	shun
t	ton
**[ʔ] in place of [t]	batman
v	van
w	win
j	yam
z	zip

**ʔ is the sound in the middle of "uh-oh".

OTHER SYMBOLS

:	Vowel sound is lengthened
~	Vowel sound is nasalized
~	introduces an alternate pronunciation of the main word

ACKNOWLEDGEMENT

This book is made possible in part with the kind support of the National Cultural Foundation's COVID Creatives Technical Assistance Grant.

Thank you for reading my book. If you enjoyed it, won't you please take a moment to leave me a review at your favorite retailer? Thanks!

Mahalia Cummins